THE B|
BOOK

VOLUME III—PART II

— GALT'S ARK —
THE BLACK SYMPHONY
Second Movement

Become Who You Are—There Are No Guarantees

Conducted by Cthulhu

The Players:
Joseph Matheny, Christopher S. Hyatt, Ph.D.
David Menafee, Ph.D., Joseph C. Lisiewski, Ph.D.
S. Jason Black, MobiusFrame

THE *Original* **FALCON PRESS**
TEMPE, ARIZONA, U.S.A.

International Standard Book Number: 978-1-935150-40-4

First Edition 2004
First Original Falcon Edition 2008

Illustrations for "Entrance Piece" by weirdpixe
All other illustrations by MobiusFrame

Address all inquiries to:
THE ORIGINAL FALCON PRESS
1753 East Broadway Road #101-277
Tempe, AZ 85282 U.S.A.

(or)
PO Box 3540
Silver Springs NV 89429 U.S.A.

website: http://www.originalfalcon.com
email: info@originalfalcon.com

The symbol you see was that of the "Extreme Individual Institute." Now that Dr. Hyatt is gone, the Institute is no more. Beware those who would assert otherwise! Beware the institutes and foundations and any other organization that purports to teach what Dr. Hyatt taught. Only Hyatt was Hyatt. No one else is, or can be.

The goal of the institute was simple: to assist extreme individuals to become who they are.

This work was for that 10% of marginal people who desire to become greater than they are now. It was not a forum or discussion or argument.

The methods of the Institute were simple: "work" in the arena of the obvious as well as the sublime. However, Dr. Hyatt was only concerned with results and not moralisms—what a person does with his power is his business.

Work was done individually via both personal contact and the internet, plus a yearly coming together done either in the physical or on the internet. There was a strict entrance exam and monthly payments were required for the operation of the Institute.

Nicholas Tharcher and Linda Miller

Cthulhu
The Conductor

by mobiusframe

ON HORNS

MAN in the WORLD

BY CHRISTOPHER S. HYATT, PH.D.

Man is born into an indifferent universe which means a universe without supernatural order. This means a world without otherworldly purpose, order, meaning, or value.

Man is a cognitive creature (not necessarily rational) whose brain both amplifies and ameliorates his fears. The amplification is both a curse—as seen in his religions and beliefs—and a blessing—as seen in his science and self-discipline.

Life is indifferent to man—sometimes dangerous, sometimes helpful—but this is not something nature intends as nature intends nothing.

The helpfulness or hostility of life is simply an interpretation from man's point of view, a result of his unique cognitive ability.

Man inherently, automatically, involuntarily and continually creates meaning—he is genetically programmed to do so. But man also has the capacity to recognize that such meaning IS his own invention and not reality. Unfortunately, most men can not and will not reconstruct their primal constructions.

This indifferent universe gives man ultimate freedom within the limitation of his own biologic nature. With this freedom comes anxiety and there is no one, or no thing, to live life for him in his place.

Man can be his own salvation—not his labels, mother, father, god, president, doctor, etc. Man's uncanny and successful ability to create otherworldly powers and then forget he has created them has saved him from extinction—as well imprisoning him in a self-created penitentiary.

To cope with his condition, man invents an otherworldly purpose (ideal categories) or, in rare cases, he can stand naked and face the chances and accidents of life using his own nature as his primary tool. He can choose to set aside the "meaning" he has created, and act based on pure (direct), uninterpreted reality (that is, respond by bypassing his categories); yet,

5

whatever reality he responds to, it is a function of the structure of his brain, nothing more nothing less.

He can develop himself into a piece of art—a standard for himself which he can admire—or he can remain an advanced "ape." Most men are nothing more than an advanced, talking ape.

A universe without a moral teleology has no purpose or order and has no moral values that man can use to interpret and order his life.

All religious, and most philosophical, interpretations of the universe and choice mechanisms are based on these constructions and are nothing but survival devices invented and policed by men and their social institutions to satisfy man's questioning brain. Hence the brain amplifies the primal issues of survival providing both an exaggerated and a calming effect.

The potentially free man must reject as pollution all sanctioned explanations of life and the moral systems based upon them. He may use them as a device when necessary but, in essence, he has trashed them.

He must accept the realities of nothing, of chance, accident, death, decay, disease and dementia and, having accomplished this through his own efforts, he has the option to attempt to discover through trial and error and by critical and often painful evaluation of his knowledge, what is valuable and useful to him.

Most men find the effort to do this too painful, too frightening, too much work, etc.—and, because they never attempt the process, they never discover the freedom it can bring, the exhilaration, the joy, the freedom afforded by knowing oneself. Those that do the necessary work of self-discovery live on a different level and speak a different language; they are often rejected by society and stand alone.

What is of value for man is what makes him happy—from eating, to sex, to adventure, to inventing, to making himself into a piece of art—and this includes discipline—for discipline gives man a greater happiness—he can be in control of himself—he is not the simple victim of chance and circumstances or sanctioned metaphysics. Feeling in control of himself through discipline and scientific discovery replaces and dissolves man's need for his preceding creations: metaphysics and religion. It requires that he continually THINK and QUESTION, and simply live with the fear generated by the realization that answers may or may not come... He no longer needs the answers so conveniently provided by metaphysics and religion.

6

Man in the world can develop a way of life that conforms to his desire to control his life. This method involves discipline, analytic thought, intuition and pleasure and is best summed up as the "risking to be man." In this way, man no longer feels a victim and, even if he is destroyed, his life is not defeated.

Thus man develops a sense of dignity and integrity by controlling the circumstances of his existence by his own active efforts—which yield him the results he desires. This I call living with style. This is what brings one the exhilarating freedom and joy possible in life.

"Normals" (est. 90% of the population) who are blind to the reality of "nothing," who live according to illusions, false values, and/or random impulses; such characters are generally either stupid and messy, idealistic and deluded, dysfunctionally self-centered and destructive. There is nothing more ugly than dysfunctional self-interest. On the other hand, *functional* self-interest (which necessitates continual self-examination, fearless acceptance of reality and willingness to act on both), not only immensely improves the quality of life of the person who practices it diligently, but also the raises the quality of the lives of those he values and who value him.

The rare individual who has recognized the reality of "nothing" and who, depending on the stage of their ability and powers, are either struggling with the fear, anxiety, and loss of control which the recognition of "nothing" brings; or who are in the process of learning the nature of dignity and integrity which are the result of discipline, using the brain, joy in living and discovery. This is man's derived and earned value-system based on authentic effort to take control of himself and his world.

BECOME WHO YOU ARE—THERE ARE NO GUARANTEES

THE ALTERNATIVE IS TO BE EITHER FALSE OR NOTHING......

What Are the Principles of Extreme Living?

BY MOBIUSFRAME

(Abstracted from *The Psychopath's Bible, The Black Books, Man in the World* and *To Lie Is Human*)

Each practitioner makes their own principles. Success, as defined by you, is the measure of the power of your principles.

PRINCIPLES OF EXTREME LIVING
AMOR FATI

Whatever occurs I will use for my best interest.

1. Advancement of the self is the highest goal.

This is the extreme part of the equation—it is in extreme opposition to the major religious and philosophical paradigms of the world. Each practitioner must define "advancement" for himself.

If one does not advance oneself, one cannot ever hope to aid others in their quest for advancement.

2. Use any means necessary to advance self—actions have consequences, most of which cannot be foreseen This is the "psychopathic" part of the equation: analytically making decisions without regard to social norms, morals, and mores is considered harmful and sick by the "establishment"... As Jung said, normal is not necessarily healthy.

3. Operate under empirical paradigms; shun metaphysics. Collect data. Make decisions based on analysis of data. Emotions, beliefs, and sentimentality have no part in decision making—unless you want them to.

4. Learn to walk through walls (do not be imprisoned by labels). Society LOVES labels—it makes it unnecessary to THINK, to do the work necessary to arrive at one's own conclusions. Accepting society's labels

allows one to avoid the ultimate fear: being shunned, rejected, or abandoned by the world; being forced to stand alone.

This is possibly the most difficult thing to do. Consider the power of labels like: SELF, mom, dad, wife, husband, priest, god, family, lover, friend, etc. (These are all substitutes for God—CSH)

5. Make yourself into a work of art: meditate, exercise, study, play, create...enjoy.

Self-advancement requires work, energy, and a certain drive—to attempt, to remain tenacious in the completion of beneficial tasks. Don't forget to play. A child inherently strives for perfection...even in play with dolls. It's fun.

6. Form your own opinions, preferences, and disposition by direct experience/observation of life—without reference to the herd. This takes the courage to risk being rejected by the herd. But the alternative is to live in falsehood, impotency and incompleteness.

Learn to think whatever/however you choose, but keep your mouth shut about it around the sheeple. Otherwise you sabotage your power.

7. Learn to blend in with the herd when desired or stand out from the herd when it serves your purpose.

8. You are born naked and alone; You will die naked and alone.

9. Everything is natural.

10. There are no guarantees.

Apply it?

The results?

XXXXXXXXXXXXXXXXXXXXXXXXXXXXXXXXXXXXXXXXXXXX
XXXXXXXXXXXXXXXXXXXXXXXXXXXXXXXXXXXXXXXXX

On Cello

Blood Relatives & Other Symbols of Death

by S. Jason Black

> That cult would never die till the stars came right again, and the secret priests would take great Cthulhu from His tomb, and revive His subjects and resume His rule of earth. The time would be easy to know, for then mankind would have become as the Great Old Ones; free, and wild, and beyond good and evil, with laws and morals thrown aside and all men shouting and killing and reveling in joy. Then the liberated Old Ones would teach them new ways to shout and kill and revel and enjoy themselves, and all the earth would flame with a holocaust of ecstasy and freedom.
> — H.P. Lovecraft, *The Call of Cthulhu*

Once, while attempting to kill my mother by black magic, I killed three other people instead.

It was later suggested to me by Dr. Hyatt, that it was impossible to curse my mother, as she had no central personality to attack. Perhaps this is so. It has been known for more than a century that the lower the intelligence of a subject, the more difficult it is to hypnotize them. Something similar may apply to magic. If no one is there, there is no target for the curse, so it goes elsewhere; in this case, my mother's relatives.

Do I have your attention? Good.

Waiting in anticipation for the death-rattle of one of the most useless people to walk the Earth, I received a 'phone call from my cousin, telling me between choking tears that her father, my mother's brother, had died the night before, pulling onto a Mississippi freeway. In front of a truck. The death occurred within seventy-two hours of the ritual. On the one hand, I was disappointed in the survival of the-thing-that-would-not-die, yet somehow uplifted that I had nailed her nearest relative. It was like having a new gun that worked beautifully, but had a sight that was only a hair off. A little adjustment, and it would be fine. I adjusted it too far the other way.

My other cousin, the oldest daughter of my mother's other brother, was abducted, raped and murdered within an hour of the conclusion of my second ceremony. It was a random abduction and no suspect has ever been arrested. The wrinkle-bag was still drawing breath, but once again the malign current had hit close to home. In the words of the late Bullwinkle Moose, "This time for sure!"

I waited until the next propitious day, which if memory serves, was Walpurgis night, I performed the ceremony again. This time, I don't know what the hell scent it was following, although there is an interesting possibility that I will pursue later. She didn't die that time either, although I thought she had once while asleep on the couch. Breathing, apparently, is unnecessary at that age. In a deep depression, I avoided answering many phone messages for about ten days, though I did write them down. Finally, I picked up the 'phone on a friend in California (I was in Missouri) and he told me he had been trying to get hold of me for ten days. He told me his ex-lover had committed suicide with some kind of downer. It happened the day following my ritual.

The interesting thing about this was that this young man had always claimed he had been psychic. A claim I never paid much attention to as he had an I.Q. approximately that of a sponge.

Astral Buttfucking

The backdrop to this is an incident that took place about a year before. I had performed an evocation which, in many ways, was a wild success. The entity attracted performed all of the clearly stated tasks to the letter, then it didn't go away. Instead, it amused itself with me, and, to my surprise, persons of my acquaintance, and persons of *their* acquaintance. This is not the appropriate place to recount in full the recurring poltergeist phenomena and other, weirder things, that continued for eight solid months. One thing that happened came back to haunt me on being informed of the aforementioned suicide. I received a telephone call one night just as I was going to bed. It was my friend. He sounded rather panicked and said there was something in the apartment.

He described seeing a figure, like a free-standing, three-dimensional figure of a man, made from hazy black smoke. I had seen something like this myself years before during an experiment in Santeria (described in *Urban Voodoo*) and had known other people over the years, some with no involvement in the esoteric or occult whatsoever, describe similar things. More recently, *Sex and Rockets,* the biography of Jack Parsons, told of a similar apparition conjured up by him and a group of fellow-travelers (including L. Ron Hubbard) in his Crowleyan magic group in California in the 1940's. So, feeling rather creepy at this point, I asked him if he had any garlic (well, what was I supposed to do?) and when the answer was no, I told him to pray, or something, and not to call again unless the furniture was flying across the room.

Sometime after midnight, the 'phone rang. While the sofas weren't flying, it was obvious from his near hysteria that *something* had happened. He said that he had been in bed, in the dark, when he felt the pressure of a body against his from behind, and assumed it was his boyfriend. Suddenly, without any preliminaries or lubrication of any kind (rude, at the very least) he was penetrated by a very large male member, moving very fast. He cried out in pain, and flailed on the bed. In doing so, he touched his boyfriend who was on the other side of the bed. He froze in terror, and the "man" disappeared. Other friends called me out of the blue during those eight months with other uncanny stories, most having no interest in such things themselves, but giving me a call because I did. I slowly came to the eerie conclusion that whether the "spirit" could read my mind or not, it was somehow capable of tracking my associations. It was Dr. Hyatt who first inclined me to this idea, as something unpleasant happened to him as well (no, no astral buttfucking) which he attributed to my "successful" working. Since that time I have read some of the older books on involvement with non-human intelligences, from Dion Fortune (the only "magician" who has much straightforward and intelligent to say on the matter, perhaps because she was a psychologist) to psychical researchers from the nineteenth century onward who examined people who made such claims of contact. The mass of modern commentary on such things from "magicians" is a melange of inept Crowleyan references to the unconscious (in spite of his claims, he knew nothing about psychology except that of manipulation, which he probably learned from his preacher father) and Jungian nonsense used to explain why your imaginary friend can't do anything for you in the real world.)

CIJ Culture

Many of the things that kill us unnecessarily are unquestioned cultural norms and superstitions that are accepted as reality even though many of them can be easily checked. Among the former—and most frequently deadly—are the supposed value of family relationships; prime among the latter are Christian-Islamic-Judaic religious values, hereafter referred to as CIJ (pronounced "keege") for short. Other things have a supernatural smell to them. These are the things Western culture *doesn't* want you to believe in, yet are real, and real enough to kill. I refer you to the bizarre stories at the beginning of this essay. One of the great myths of European society, and its retarded stepchild, America, is that curses (or good luck spells) only work if the person they are directed at believes in them. There is a psychological phenomena—formulated circa the 1940's–60's—called "Voodoo death," which involves the death of a person who has been informed of being the subject of a death curse. They are informed, one way or another, and the autonomic nervous system overreacts to such a degree that it kills them.

Unfortunately, as has been pointed out many times, in a society that believes in magic, anyone who finds out they are cursed would immediately go to another magician to have the spell counteracted. It would, therefore, behoove the sorcerer to keep his work a secret. There is also an old saying in the Caribbean islands that there is no easier target for a spell than a white man who doesn't believe in magic. It must be said, however, that in places like Haiti, or in communities where Santeria or Macumba are practiced, both methods are sometimes used.

Among the tiny minority of "wiccans" or "Crowlyites" that I have met who genuinely practiced magic to influence real-time events, the ones who have talked openly about their experiments have confirmed that the basic rules of witchcraft, which are identical throughout the world, seem to hold true. Informing your target of the spell, is not one of them.

The Lover Who Wouldn't Go Away

I once had a friend who had an unrequited love for some young woman. He had been told of my interest in magic (I had already co-authored *Urban Voodoo* and had earned the nickname "Voodoo" from my local friends. No respect.) and asked me for a love charm. I had gone down that road myself before and knew what it might hold in store, but doing it for another person, especially one so well-balanced, seemed all right. And besides, I was interested in the experiment.

I prepared a talisman from one of the traditional grimoires, presented him with it at a pre-arranged meeting, and told him what to say over it and how to consecrate it with his own blood. He was to place this somewhere where she would pass over it or be very near it daily. That was the last that I saw of him for nearly six months. When I saw him again, he looked a little too eager to see me. He told me that he had planted the talisman between her mattress and box springs after following my instructions, and waited for results. (She was living with him when I gave him the talisman, but she didn't "love" him, had her own room, and was about to leave.) At first, he said, her feelings not only revived, but she said she was head-over-heels in love with him. Things went great for three months or so and then turned strange. She became less and less interested in sex but still maintained her intense love for him. Finally she said she didn't want to have sex any more but loved him and wanted to stay with him. He was sure she wasn't seeing anyone else. She had no intention of leaving or of willingly let him see anyone else. What should he do? Retrieve the talisman and destroy it, I replied. He couldn't. Her bedroom had it's own lock, and since he planted it, he hadn't had a single chance to get the damn thing. And that's the last that I ever heard of it. I questioned him carefully, and he never said anything to the girl.. I knew, since I made the talisman, that the odds were overwhelmingly against her recognizing it if she found it. So much for suggestion.

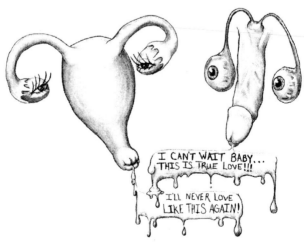

14

Heil Hitler

The Nazi involvement with the occult has become legendary since the publication of *The Morning of the Magicians* in the early 1960's and *The Spear of Destiny* a decade later. The former book is a sincere examination of historical weirdness by two Frenchmen with backgrounds in science; the second, which I dearly wanted to believe when I first read it, has a very large proportion of bunk mixed in with authentic history. The proportion of rubbish to fact, I eventually came to find, was so great that one knowledgeable critic declared it a novel. But back to the real Nazis. In one of the most famous stories told about Hitler he is quoted as saying, "The superman already exists. I have seen him, and I was afraid." He would also wake up at night in terror, ring for an attendant and point to an empty corner of the room and gasp, "There! There! He is there! Do you see him?" No one ever seems to have. If one researches the evidence for human–non-human interaction across the various fields of thought, from religion to the periphery of science, to first-hand accounts from acquaintances (which, if you start to make known your interest, you will find are alarmingly numerous) it becomes very convincing. It also adds a chilling perspective on some segments of history such as that of Nazi Germany, and the religious war we have begun to be engaged in. It should be noted that as of this writing, America has what is probably its first genuine born-again President. This is something that I originally couldn't believe, considering his sophisticated family background, until he appointed as Attorney General a man whose beliefs I am painfully familiar with from years of listening to fundamentalist radio. Believe me, if the American public in general knew what these men thought, their hair would turn white. Or at least have an attractive blue rinse.

Our CIJ culture has had a millennium to perfect verbal defenses against treating with anything that might communicate—except its imaginary friend Jesus. In earlier times there were physical retributions, but these have now been mostly internalized. Yet, if one pays attention, it becomes clear that even that emptiest of religions, Christianity, has in its midst people who have had what seem to be genuine contacts with something-or-other. Most, however, are merely having nervous breakdowns.

Drugs, Detergent & Hypnosis

While the use of drugs to accomplish such a thing might, with some justification, be called into question in modern times, nevertheless, there are people whose opinions must be taken seriously. One of the most notable is the late Dr. John Lilly, whose experiments with porpoises made him world famous. But before Flipper, there were other experiments with mind-altering drugs. These were genuine experiments, not the slang term "experiment" as in "experiment with sex." Lilly was educated in a tradition, frowned upon even then, where it was considered justifiable for a researcher to test an experimental drug upon himself. Now, as far as I know, this is entirely *verboten*. In any case, he was in a hotel room one evening, and prepared to inject himself with whatever drug it was whose effects he was trying to codify. Just what that was isn't important as he either picked up the wrong syringe or had forgotten to prepare it. He injected himself with what he described as "detergent foam." If this is literally what it was, he was lucky he didn't have an embolism! It sent him into a very bad place, possibly near death. But right at the height (or nadir) of the experience, he entered a state of calm—the room disappeared around him, and he found himself in a chamber, or space, where two beings stood in front of him and identified themselves as aliens. After a conversation with them (which you may read for yourself in *The Center of the Cyclone*) he awoke, in some physical distress, but otherwise fine. It could be dismissed easily as a chemically induced hallucination but Lilly, a trained observer, admitted in his book that he was unsure. After consideration (and it was some time between the experiments and the writing of the book), he said it had unique qualities he had not experienced on LSD or other chemicals, and so, considered the possibility that somehow, for some reason, it was real. A brave thing for a man with a professional reputation to protect to say in print.

In addition, there is Terrence McKenna, a man considered an expert on psychedelic mushrooms, who also claims to have talked to aliens (or something) while under the influence. In addition, he suggests that psychedelic plants may have given a boost to early man's brain development. They are still used sacramentally in many religions. He also points out that animals (e.g., horses), are known to deliberately seek out plants like datura. McKenna also asserts that psychedelic experience were far more important in the development of human history than has generally been realized. This, of course, is partly due to the nature of the historians, and partly due to a vast ignorance of the organic sources of the substances themselves throughout much of Western history—except for secret societies like the Witches (the real ones, not the modern imitation) and the one that the painter Hieronymous Bosch is said to have belonged to. Which, in his case, explains a lot.

We have already entered an era long predicted by so-called "futurists" of an increasing gap between those with knowledge—"*gnosis*" in the broadest sense—and the common herd. This gap has always been there, but now, thanks to the computer explosion, is in the embryonic stages of producing a potentially violently divided society. I am not talking about rioting in the streets, although that may come, too. I am referring to a growing class hostility motivated by something other than economics (although there will be an element of that), but by gut-level hostility which can escalate to crime on an individual level, and the very correct perception that the world is falling apart. I am referring primarily here to religionists, but it applies even to the totally irreligious whose view of things is locked into a time already past. This is exemplified by that triad of stupidity, CIJ. Those who wish to survive, much less thrive, in this environment must proactively embrace attitudes and technologies for living they might not want known to their friends, family and neighbors.

Among these are "alternative" (which often means "foreign") medicines and methods of bodily maintenance which the general-practice M.D. might frown upon (I have never personally met a family-practice doctor who knew about anything but B–12, but I know they are out there).

Yoga and self-hypnosis (the existence of the latter is still denied in a distinctly paranoid way by some doctors) both have extensive backgrounds of Western research, that of hypnosis going back to the late eighteenth century. Having practiced both of these for going on twenty years, I can attest to the fact that the saying is easier than the doing, and there are few activities that will demonstrate just how thoroughly you already are hypnotized than beginning these techniques. An excellent overall history of hypnosis can be found in *Trance* by Brian Ingliss (Paladin, 1990).

Sex, Sperm & Blood

The disciplining, *NOT* repression, of sex is something which even people whom I have met that are more sexually enthusiastic than normal find almost impossible to do. The use of sex, in conjunction with yoga and ritual activities, produces startling results well beyond the physical, even beyond those that could be considered "kundalini" phenomena. I have had—and known others who have had—experiences that could only be described as paranormal in conjunction with the sexual addition to ritual. Make no mistake, these efforts are not "fun." They require either abstain-

17

ing from orgasm by the male, or the concentration upon an image or goal during orgasm. It also requires scheduling according to astrological and ritual requirements, which kind of kills spontaneity. There are outlines of such practices in *Pacts With the Devil* (Black & Hyatt, New Falcon) and in the "secret" sexual techniques of Aleister Crowley, as well as *Secrets of Western Tantra* (Hyatt, New Falcon) and *Tantra Without Tears* (Hyatt & Black, New Falcon). In reference specifically to Crowley's "secret" sex technique (in reality a standard Hindu Tantra method) a heterosexual couple has sex in whatever way they want, but the orgasm must be had with the penis inserted into the vagina. During climax, both parties must visualize the desired result (although Crowley admitted that he had practiced this technique without the partner knowing), and the male then consumes his own sperm as a sacrament. Crowley erroneously identified this as alchemy. It has been commented that this was, in reality, an expression of Crowley's homosexuality (during homosexual sex magic Crowley apparently played the passive role). Any experienced prostitute would probably agree. While he was eating his own sperm from a vagina he had just fucked, it is likely that in his imagination he was consuming someone *else's* sperm. There are, of course, methods of homosexual sex magic. The basic technique described above can be adapted with some flourishes. Ignoring the nonsense of consuming your own sperm, the primary use of sexual fluids and, indeed, blood in magic is the consecration of talismans.

Vampires Blow

Both blood and sexual fluids are considered as vectors for the lifeforce. Like so many things in magic, this is sometimes considered to be symbolic—but it may be literally true as blood and semen are chemically almost identical, which might explain the use of oral sex in Tantrik vampirism. In this practice, the person performing the oral activity refrains from orgasm and concentrates on the lifeforce entering his/her system and remaining there. While vampirism is disappointingly more difficult in reality than in the movies, some distinctly weird phenomena seem connected to it. The few people I have known who have tried this (those, that is, whose stories I trust), have described uncomfortable physical and psychic states, and sometimes odd reactions in their sex partners, apparently including unwanted telepathic contact. Rarely did they receive the desired benefits. There seems to be a *real* secret to this that can probably be found in hard-to-find Tantrik and Taoist texts.

The most nearly classic story I know came from someone who was a student of the occult, and came to Southern California in the late 1970's. Exploring the sexual wonderfulness of Los Angeles at the time, he began to frequent bathhouses on Saturday nights. One time he decided to try the sex vampirism experiment, and took a young man to his room. Giving the best blowjob he knew how, he allowed the other guy to come in his mouth while avoiding following suit. Upon closing the door behind his departing friend, he heard a thud in the hall outside. He opened the door to check, and discovered his young man flat on the floor. When asked if he was all right, the young man said, "I don't know what happened. Suddenly I got dizzy and fell." He assumed the experiment worked, and so do I. However, he freely admitted that he got no noticeable benefit from it, and said he thought it must have "leaked."

A couple of years later, this same person had moved to Hollywood, at that time a wonderful maelstrom of vice. He met someone, an Oriental man, with whom he began the same experiment over a period of time, this time with a few flourishes. For example, he saved a condom used by the man as a "magical link." During the approximately two months of this activity, while his partner never collapsed on him, he himself developed weird symptoms. He went into spontaneous trance-states that he described as, not hypnotic, but almost psychedelic. He also developed a constant and totally useless precognitive faculty. Useless in that he could see things about five minutes before they happened. A fender-bender in the street, or a skunk rounding a corner (skunks are endemic in that part of Hollywood)—that kind of thing. When the activity stopped, the phenomena stopped. At this time he had no experience in yoga or hypnotic states and this may be the reason for the useless unpredictability, and yet, the description reminds me of similar descriptions of "siddis" or magical powers developed in connection with kundalini yoga. At least the skunk predictor was useful.

In all, in spite of the number of people who would like to be vampires, it seems to take discipline and knowledge of particularly obscure occult techniques. It is probably a salutary exercise to attempt to vampirize your neighbors. There is no need to blow them.

Solitary Magic

The techniques of solitary magic are basically the same as those mentioned above, only solitary. It is usually used in the charging of a talisman or to conjure up desired results. This involves the same difficulties as before, involving correct concentration during orgasm, although to a lesser degree..

Select the appropriate day and hour for the work (the hour will vary from day to day; the necessary information can be acquired from the table in *Pacts With The Devil* or most classic grimoires), prepare whatever tools, talismans or altar are needed, and then begin with an period of raja yoga (or the equivalent trance technique), and then perform whatever ritual you decide is appropriate. This could be something like a Black Mass. When the time comes for the sex portion, you may pause and use whatever means required to arouse yourself. If this means watching *Debbie Does Saskatchewan*, so be it. The orgasm should not be the end of the ritual, which should be ended with dignity—with *Debbie* turned off. If the rules are followed, the accompanying phenomena (if they occur) will rarely have a negative backlash. It should be repeated, however, and for any serious goal; about a month should be allowed for, the ritual being performed at least twice a week. One drawback: your talisman may become a little crusty.

The considered and focused use of fantasies to free yourself from environmental norms. computer material, pornography, odd old movies, can be used in conjunction with Tantrik techniques and self-hypnosis to great effect. For example, turn on *The Today Show,* and masturbate while watching Katie Couric. This exercise is therapeutic for both men and women. If you are doing this exercise with a lover or spouse you must not have coitus. You must both concentrate on Katie. Katie is Kali.

The Ones From Elsewhere

The myth of something coming back to "get" us—or help us—seems to go back, in one form or another, forever. This has been extremely empowering, in *both* its good and evil forms, to the CIJ mentality in the twentieth century. The exponentially increasing religious psychosis in America and the Middle East is a prime example. On the other side of the coin, the "alien" myth (however grounded on fact it may be) has had a strong influence on recent generations. The Cthulhu Mythos of H.P. Lovecraft, which started out as an elaborate fiction by a brilliant writer, has evolved into a subterranean occult religion which expresses itself not only in books on magic and the occult like the various bogus *Necronomicons*, but in role-playing games, idols to worship and sacrifice your family to, a place in modern Satanism and a subset of Crowleyanity, to movies (most, except *The Dunwich Horror*, very bad) to a website entitled "Cthulhu Wants You!" This myth is roughly based on the old Book of Enoch/fallen angel routine, which makes it, on a deep level easier to segue into than the originally hopeful, but ultimately pathetic neopagan movement.

Since the majority of people who have requested the *Black Books* have already rejected the philosophical core of current society, I feel at ease stating outright that Satanism or, more properly, Luciferianism, is Christian Tantrism. It is all that is left of the Gnosticism of the early Church. Lame as LaVey's Church of Satan was, it was still an open statement of defiance. Wicca and Crowlyanity, giving their members an out, have allowed them to return to their childhood programming while claiming rejection. The primary goal of almost all esoteric systems of self-development is the overcoming of training by incompetent families. Abortion, genetic manipulation and brain change are all justifiable methods to use in the fight for self-actuation. Unfortunately, this effort all too often takes the bulk of a lifetime.

Finally, to quote, or misquote, or something, a recent remark of Dr. Hyatt's, "Brain change is the only way to escape your programming. Brain damage is brain change. Therefore, brain damage is good."

So go ahead, *buy* that new butt plug, pick up that 1.5 liters of vodka, and think of Katie.

Oh, and if you are Jewish, here is something really easy. Go out to dinner with some senior members of your family and order pork.

On Bass

The Production of Complex Organic Molecules
by Radio-Frequency Electrical Discharges

BY JOSEPH C. LISIEWSKI, PH.D.
INSTITUTE FOR THE EXPERIMENTAL INVESTIGATION
OF THE ORIGIN OF LIFE (IEIOL)

This work advocates that life may have originated on earth through the influence of electromagnetic forces produced by lightning discharges in a primordial reducing atmosphere. Early research [1] concentrated upon the electric component of the discharge and yielded the basic building blocks of matter: amino acids. This presentation focuses upon lightning-generated electromagnetic fields as the causal agent of higher-ordered organic synthesis. It postulates that certain electromagnetic frequencies naturally favour biological synthesis. To test this idea, magnetic and radio frequency fields were applied to such atmospheres resulting in the synthesis of not only amino acids, but also peptides and polypeptides, complex compounds produced only by living matter.

Introduction

In 1953, Stanley L. Miller [1] passed a 60 kV radio frequency discharge current of approximately 500 kHz through an apparatus (Figure 1) that contained a water vapor and reducing atmospheric gas mixture. This "reducing atmosphere," also referred to as a "primordial," "prebiotic," or "primitive" atmosphere, consisted of methane, ammonia, and hydrogen. There was no free oxygen present. Water vapor from the boiling flask (lower left) passed into a 5 litre flask (top right) equipped with a set of wire electrodes. The spark discharge across the gap simulated the lightning discharges that were believed to have raked the primordial atmosphere for tens of millions of years, giving rise to organic compounds that "somehow" organized themselves into living matter. The water component of the reaction condensed back into a liquid after passing through a watercooled condenser. From there it moved through the U-tube pictured, and flowed back into the boiling flask. This gaseous-water vapor mix was recirculated nonstop for seven days. What Miller produced in this experiment stunned the scientific world: amino acids, the basic building blocks of all life on earth.

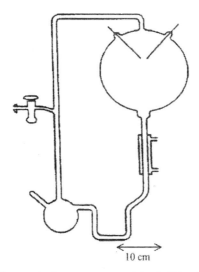

Figure 1. Apparatus used by Miller [1]

This accomplishment gave rise to several scientific organizations devoted exclusively to the scientific study of the Origin of Life issue. Throughout a 28-year period, Miller's work was replicated many times. Variations in the velocity of the gas flow, rearrangement of the components of the apparatus, types of discharges, variations in gaseous constituents, etc., were tried in an effort to synthesize more complex organic compounds needed for living matter to arise naturally in this primordial earth environment, e.g., peptides and polypeptides which are

23

long chains of amino acids, linked together in biological fashion. Apart from some interesting results that mimicked larger organic compounds, no substantial progress was made, however, towards answering the fundamental question of how life arose on earth.

By the early 1980's, work on the electric (lightning-simulated) discharge and its associated phenomena was abandoned, and emphasis shifted away from this fundamental question. Instead, the scientific societies' involved became interested in such related activities as DNA-RNA artificial synthesis. From the 1990's to the present, their focus shifted again; this time, to the speculation of how life may have been transported to earth by meteoric and cometary bombardment. For all practical purposes then, the attack on the fundamental problem has been abandoned by the scientific community at large and remains as such today.

An Impetus to Experiment

For the past thirty-four years the author has been engaged in this field of scientific exploration. He has proposed a new theoretical model that attempts to further an answer to the fundamental question, and has tested it in the laboratory. This new model arose from several factors, including an analysis of Miller's original paper [1]. This study indicated that, of the numerous variables tested in his experiments, the most important were the means by which lightning phenomena was simulated.

Principally, as mentioned previously, Miller used a continuous radio frequency (RF) discharge. In addition, however, a pulsed direct current source was also used to simulate electrostatic charge buildup between adjacent clouds, or between cloud and ground. Lastly, a continuous AC electric discharge of 15,000 volts, provided by a transformer, was also employed. The RF discharge produced the most fruitful results: about 1 gram of organic compounds after a week's continuous sparking. Among the important amino acids produced were glycine, d,l-alanine, β–alanine, d,l-α–amino-n-butyric acid, sarcosine, and α–aminoisobutyric acid. The AC discharge produced about one-third this quantity, while the pulsed DC discharge yielded a smaller production of glycine only.

The internal pressure of the apparatus was maintained at < 1.5 atmospheres and Miller speculated that higher pressures might decrease the time required for organic compound production. Due to these and other chemical factors presented in his paper, Miller concluded that amino acids and the more important compounds of living systems would be formed in the solution phase as opposed to the gas phase (and discharge site) of the system. This latter and crucial view was supported by the lack of urea in the experimental results he obtained.

A New Theoretical Model

A new model that attempts to explain the mechanism of complex molecule formation is presented in [2] but is too extensive for inclusion here.

The essential feature of the model is that the frequency of the discharge energy input is a critical component of synthesis: not just the magnitude of the energy itself.

Electrically charged byproducts of the discharge, in particular protons, will have a magnetic dipole moment associated with them due to their intrinsic spin. In the presence of a magnetic field these dipoles will precess at the Larmor frequency and superposition of an RF electromagnetic field can induce resonance effects that aid alignment of the bonds between the discharge products. This increases the probability of the formation of long-chain molecules.

The lightning discharge is harmonically rich and, in addition to low frequency magnetic fields associated with bulk current flow, radio frequency fields will also be present. This gives rise to the possibility that the resonance conditions outlined above could have arisen naturally in the lightning discharge process, and could be the actual mechanism by which higher ordered organic synthesis occurred on primordial earth. The apparatus used by the author (Figure 2) attempts to simulate the conditions under which such synthesis may occur.

The pressure in Miller's apparatus was of order 1.5 atmospheres. Differing cosmological views suggests that the pressure on prebiotic earth was higher than this and may have played a role in organic synthesis. The author believes this was indeed the case and his apparatus operated at 2.0 atmospheres.

In addition the apparatus was designed so that the water vapour entered the reaction site immediately and directly as a comparison of the two figures will illustrate.

Experimental Procedure

The synthesis chamber used in the present investigation is shown in Figure 2 and consists of three sections: the bottom "water chamber," the central "synthesis chamber," and the top "allyn condenser." It was made of Pyrex, 914 mm in length, with an O.D. of 70 mm and an I.D. of 63.5 mm, giving a volume of order 2.9×10^{-3} m³. The desired increased pressure (~2 atmospheres) in the system is an inevitable condition of the closed system, while the placement of the condenser on top of the synthesis chamber guarantees a high water vapor pressure at the reaction site. Gentle heating (just below boiling) provided by an electrically-regulated heating tape, allowed the water and gas molecules to circulate in the region of the discharge for a longer period of time, as compared to Miller's system. Water flow through the condenser was about 30 cm³ s⁻¹ at 16–20°C⬜⬜Lightning discharges were simulated in all nine experiments with a 50 kV RF Tesla coil of nominal frequency 500 kHz. Due to electric dissociation of the methane and ammonia gases by the discharge, resulting in the production of free hydrogen, only these two gases were added in equal volume.

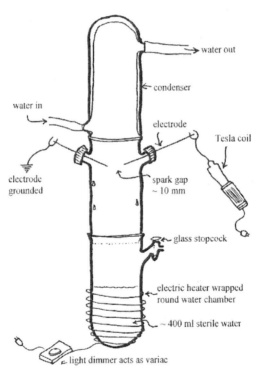

Figure 2. Present Synthesis Chamber [2]

Fixed magnets provided field strengths of 390 and 950 gauss, which changed the Larmor precessional frequency for protons from 1.65 MHz in the first case, to 4.02 MHz in the second case. Using this design and conditions, it was found experimentally that only fifteen hours of operation (as opposed to seven days) were needed to produce the results achieved. The precessional frequency induced by the fixed magnets was matched by an RF frequency provided by a radio frequency generator that was used to superimpose a second RF field at right angles to the magnets. The RF supply drove a coil affixed to the outside of the apparatus and parallel to the discharge site (not shown in Figure 2). Power dissipation into the synthesis site provided by the generator was 120–150 mW. Careful regulation of the water temperature below the boiling point is important to prevent excessive pressure in the chamber.

Discussion of Results

All runs yielded the same amino acids as obtained by Miller but a number of others were also identified, including isoleucine, serine, tyrosine, glutamic acid and aspartic acid, as analyzed by TLC (thin layer chromatography) methods.

In addition to the amino acids produced, polypeptides on the order of $1-2 \times 10^{-3}$ g cm^3 were produced in 5 runs using the 390 gauss magnetic field, with larger amounts on the order of 7×10^{-3} g cm^3 produced with the 950 gauss field and the EM coil operating at 1.6 MHz. In contrast, the run using a 500 kHz discharge with the 950 gauss field only produced 2×10^{-3} g cm^{-3} of polypeptides demonstrating that the frequency of the applied field has a pronounced effect on the polypeptide generation. Polypeptide and peptide analysis was accomplished through the use of a Hitachi 911 Auto Chemical Analyzer (HACA).

The addition of elemental sulfur to two runs yielded only peptides. Sulfur possibly competed for binding sites with the peptides formed, preventing the formation of the higher-ordered compounds. Peptide production resulting from the 390 gauss field at 500 kHz was measured at $1-3 \times 10^{-3}$ g cm^3 with the increased amounts being produced for the 950 gauss field and the coil operating at 1.6 MHz.

The above results demonstrate that the radio frequency electric fields associated with lightning discharges occurring on primordial earth played a more significant role in the generation of those compounds needed for life to arise, than was formerly thought possible. Interested parties should

27

contact the author for a free copy of, "Theoretical and Laboratory Procedures in the Origin of Life Issue," which gives detailed theory and experimental information that will allow full replication of the results discussed.

References

[1] H. Urey, S. Miller, "Production of Some Organic Compounds Under Possible Primitive Earth Conditions", *Journal of the American Chemical Society,* Volume 77, 2351–2361, 1954.

[2] J.C. Lisiewski, "Possible Electrodynamic Mechanisms Underlying the Origin of Living Systems", Doctoral Thesis, The Union Institute, Cincinnati, Ohio, 1998.

On Piano

The Christian Destruction of the Mysteries

By David Menafee, Ph.D.

When Saul of Tarsus came to Ephesus, it marked the beginning of an all-out assault on traditional religion in the Mediterranean, and an aggressive campaign to undermine the Mysteries by which every generation was attuned to the dynamic processes of the Earth. Ephesus now lies in ruins along the western coast of Turkey. But in the days of Saul it was one of the major cities of the Roman Empire, an economic and cultural hub dominated by veneration of the multi-breasted, fecund goddess Artemis. To a modern reader, it may seem strange that a *virgin* goddess should embody fertility for millions of worshipers. But the whole point was the enormous power of creating life that women and women alone possessed and controlled. Saul, who was quoted as saying women should be wholly subservient to men and not even speak in public, obviously held a dim view of such elevation of womanhood as the Artemis cult represented. His attitude was noted by the local population, who poured into the streets to protest his attack on their civil institutions, with cries of "Artemis is Great!"

Saul was a zealous sort. He had been zealous as a Pharisaic Jew attacking the new Christian movement, and he became just as zealous as a Christian attacking Pharisaic Judaism, which he now declared totally invalid. He was subject to seizures, during which he had what he considered direct communications from the spirit world. These convinced him not only to join the new Christian movement, but to direct it out of Judaism into direct engagement with followers of non-Jewish spirituality. You can search through every word ascribed to Yeshu the Galilean, and find

29

not a single remark directed against forms of worship outside of Judaism. His Nazorean movement seems to have been primarily an internal reform of Jewish practices. But Saul felt himself instructed to "evangelize" the non-Jewish world. He dropped his Jewish name and took the Roman name Paulus, and began to travel from city to city spreading the "good news," which could be boiled down to four noble truths:

1. God is not in the world as a living force, but created the world apart from himself. The world therefore is alienated from the divine and has no value. The forces of nature are not divine, but demonic.

2. The physical body is corrupt and separate from the true person. The processes of sex, birth, and death are not a blessing but a curse marked by mortality.

3. God has created this world for destruction, and allows bad things to happen within it as a "test." The spiritual forces that respond to people's worldly concerns for life, love, safe childbirth, health, safe travel, prosperity, and success are therefore also demonic, not divine.

4. All that one should care about is escaping this world for a heaven where one is not plagued by the processes of life and death, not bothered by plants or animals, but spends a sexless eternity praising God.

"Paul" brought from his Jewish heritage the idea that there was only one God, a great and wrathful patriarch with a serious case of Narcissism. There was no room left within this rigid monotheism for a goddess, or for any of the natural processes of birth and generation that necessarily require feminine assistance. The one God creates by giving orders and the occasional hands-on craftsmanship. Creation is a set of distinct objects molded by God's whim, not a web of interconnected being.

People did to Paul what just about anyone would do to someone who went around shouting that everyone was a fool, that the gods did not exist, that the principal traditions of the people were wicked — they beat the crap out of him, several times. The local police often hauled him away for disturbing the peace and inciting riot — often for his own protection. This was, of course, "persecution," even at a time when there was no constitutional right to free speech. There was, however, freedom of religion in the Roman Empire.

Modern textbooks immured in Christian bias wildly distort this fact, and regularly depict Rome as a trial-run for Nazi Germany. The truth is, Roman society was such a model of enlightened governance that it was taken as the primary model for the United States when it was founded.

The Romans believed in keeping government small. An army was needed to protect people from invaders and gangs, basically to defend "the Roman way of life." Since the army needed to be paid, taxes had to be collected. If people paid their taxes and kept the peace, they could do anything else they liked. They could spend every day in a temple, or every day in a bordello. They could believe what they wanted, and follow a personal ethical code of their choice, so long as it did not infringe on anyone else's right to life, liberty and the pursuit of happiness. Every once in awhile someone would get into power with some peculiar notions of giving the government a bigger hand in everyday life. But such experiments at "social engineering" were short-lived—usually as short-lived as the person who tried to make them law. The Empire was also very cosmopolitan, with people of every race and color living side by side in the cities, each with as much opportunity as the next person to rise high in business, culture, or government.

Freedom of religion in the Roman Empire was qualified in two ways. First, technically there was no separation of religion and government. The government supervised religious institutions, making sure no one made off with the temple funds. It also sponsored religion with tax money, pretty even-handedly. This made sense because temples were the center of civil life. They sponsored feasts, festivals, parades, theater, local building projects, and charity. So they were the best avenue for the government to use to invest in the cities, which were, of course, the government's political base. Second, in a small town or village, one's spiritual options were somewhat limited. "The family that prays together stays together" was a common sentiment, and that idea extended to the whole community. Only in the big cities was there enough diversity for people to experiment with something other than the faith of their mothers. The big cities were precisely Paul's targeted mission field for this reason, and from the very beginning the Christians were accused of being a cult that broke up families and undermined traditional values.

Paul's method is familiar to anyone who knows how new religions and cults work. He claimed to have direct revelations from the true God. And his verbal attack on traditional values—combined with dire warnings of a dark future—shook his audience's confidence that they were on the right path in life. Anyone who approached Paul and his team with interest was flooded with love, generosity, and a feeling of belonging. At the same time, Paul instructed the new recruit to stop participating in normal social life: to not attend public festivals or other social functions connected to his or her old way of life, and not to see friends, family, and neighbors. The Christians formed a "new family," in which everyone was a "brother" or "sister." The new recruit would be constantly accompanied by these spiritual kin, to be monitored and encouraged in the new way of life. Any serious breach would be met with curses and shunning from the group until he or she repented. The way of looking at nature and the world's value taught in the mysteries was systematically drummed out of the recruit's mind. Past ethical principles and values were declared worthless, and the person was put through an initiation designed to induce spirit-possession. The new spirit was thought to take possession of a person's mind, and guide him or her instinctively to behave in conformity with the Christian message. Believers were kept in a constant state of fervor and anxiety by the message that the world would be destroyed any day, and only true believers would be rescued. They quit their jobs, broke engagements to marry, and met in all-night sessions of prophecy and speaking in tongues. Some were so driven to distraction by the delay of the world's end that they sought to force it by setting fire to Rome itself. Thousands were killed as the poorer sections of the city were reduced to ashes. Several Christian ringleaders, no doubt along with a handful of innocent bystanders, were rounded up and publicly executed by the state. Another "great persecution."

The original followers of Yeshu the Galilean, led by his brother Yaqob, were appalled at Paul's practices. They sent their own missionaries wherever Paul had been to undo some of the damage and let people know the actual content of Yeshu's message of love and non-violence. We don't know exactly how Paul's version of the religion prevailed, but it did. Perhaps it is the simple fact that fanaticism always has an advantage over tolerance because it does not rule out any tactic in advancing its goals. Paul's success set Christianity on a path of violent confrontation with the Mysteries.

Within a hundred years of Paul's activities, Christianity had become a notorious cult. People had had enough exposure to Christians to understand what they were all about. They were quite simply "atheists," who did not believe in the gods who filled the world and governed all of its life-sustaining energies. And because service to the gods was a collective responsibility, one bad apple in a village could profane the sacred realm, and break the partnership with the gods on which everyday life depended. This was viewed as a direct threat to everyone's well-being. Naturally, then, people took matters into their own hands to harass, drive out, and even lynch an atheist Christian. In cities where the rule of law prevailed, those Christians who publicly profaned and flaunted the sacred were arrested. If they recanted their hatred of the gods, they were pardoned. If they persisted, they were executed. This quickly devolved into ritual suicide on the part of the Christians, who deliberately incited arrest and prosecution to more quickly escape the evil world. Of all the things pondered by the penetrating mind of Marcus Aurelius, this willful suicide and disdain for life was something he said he could not fathom.

This whole period is perversely called the time of the "Apologists" by Christian historians, who claim that Christian leaders sought to explain themselves politely to the surrounding society. The few "Apologies" that survive from this time paint a very different picture. Even though they ask for Christians to be protected by the state from their neighbors, they include virulent attacks on the beliefs and values of those neighbors, declaring everything they believe and do to be foolish and false. These documents also represent a new phase in the Christian war, specifically on the Mysteries. In the Second and early Third centuries, Christian writers began to publicly profane the Mysteries by revealing the secret experiences one had when initiated into them. Since many of these Christian writers had converted from traditional religion, they had actually gone through the Mysteries, and vowed never to speak or even hint about their content. Now they violated their oaths and sought to ridicule the Mystery experience by mentioning certain things that went on there totally out of context.

The Mysteries, you see, were not a set of teachings, a laundry list of ideas, or merely a ritual procedure. The Mysteries worked as total experiences in which the initiate's mind is prepared and carefully manipulated into intuitively perceiving the significance of sights, sounds, smells, tastes, and sensations that in ordinary experience and the plain light of day would be perfectly ordinary. The so-called "Apologists" of Christianity, now de-programmed from their Mystery initiation, disassembled its constituent parts and ridiculed them as "all there is to the Mysteries." Since modern historians mostly rely on such sources to reconstruct the mysteries, there has been a serious problem grasping their inner meaning. Fortunately, there are threads of this meaning running through the spiritual traditions that became embedded in later forms of religion, and the discerning eye can see connections to the fragments of direct evidence about the Mysteries.

The profaning of the Mysteries started to have serious consequences for Mediterranean society. People follow fads. They mindlessly repeat things they have heard without thinking about them for themselves. And new generations love to tear down the old ways, just for the sake of rebellion. People got a kick out of dismissing something their elders took oh so seriously. Despite being an illegal gang bent on the destruction of the state and society, Christianity attracted a following. The society started to come apart. Christians tapped into class tensions. They recruited heavily in the army where young men were far from home. While attacking the Mithra Mysteries popular with soldiers, they copied some of its ritual forms to maintain the atmosphere of a familiar club. And whenever they could, they committed public acts of impiety and desecration. Inevitably, the gods abandoned Rome. The Empire collapsed internally and externally. Invaders pillaged hundreds of cities. The great Roman army split into factions and devastated the countryside. The leaders called for everyone to return to the gods, to make offerings and pray for peace and safety once again. Some Christians sought public suicide once again. Others, more comfortable with worldly success, bribed government officials to issue false certificates of sacrifice that they could wave in front of their neighbors while pretending to be on the same side. The campaigns of traditional piety did nothing to reverse the collapse of civil society. And so, in desperation, the leaders of Roman society turned to a dictator to restore stability.

Diocletian is another one of those Emperors who has gone down in history as a great "persecutor" of the Christians. What is forgotten was that he was a persecutor of just about everyone. He decided to balance the state budget on the backs of the temples. He cut off government support for all temples outside of the four imperial cities and, by greatly increasing taxes, he drained the resources that might have supported the temples locally. Since traditional religion had always been closely interrelated to civil government, first locally, then nationally, then imperially, Diocletian's policy was an amputation at the neck for all traditional religion in the Empire. He hated everything "un-Roman," and confiscated the operating accounts of Egyptian, Syrian, Phrygian, and Celtic temples. He ordered the execution of any missionary bringing spiritual teachings from outside the Empire, from Persia or India. Finally, he turned on the Christians, confiscating their money and property, burning their books, and sending their leaders off to labor camps. In doing so, he did Christianity a big favor. Since he was so widely hated by such a huge segment of the population, his antagonism made Christianity popular. Isis worshipers ambushed police convoys to free Christian prisoners. For a brief time of common adversity, people of many different religions made common cause. This mood prevailed in the years following Diocletian, and led to the rise of Constantine the Great.

Once again the history books, deep in Christian bias, have it wrong. Constantine was not "the first Christian Emperor," and he did not "make Christianity the state religion." These are fictions meant to push the victory of Christianity back in time. Constantine was an initiate of the Mithra Mysteries, and a devotee of the Unconquerable Sun, Sol Invictus. He was, in fact, an early practitioner of what today we would call "New Age" religion, because he felt that all religions contain parts of the same truth, and he selected the most appealing features of each and wove them into a personal faith of his own. The Christians, like everyone else, received official acceptance, and for the first time were considered members of a religion, rather than a socially destructive atheist secret society. Astute Christian leaders cooperated with Constantine in guiding the movement towards mainstream status. That meant they needed temples, priests, public worship, holy days, and multiple forms of the divine to appeal to. At this moment, in the early Fourth century, Christianity adopted all of these things, and began to look like a respectable religion. For the first time, they demarcated areas of sacred space and furnished them as if they were temples with standard sacrificial rites. They imitated traditional ritual, imagery, and music, and dressed their leaders in the robes of priestcraft. They adopted the common concept of a triune divine family of transcendent Father, immanent Mother, and beloved Son, adapting it by replacing the Mother with a sexless divine Spirit. When this failed to appear to the masses, they promoted Mary as the new form of the Mother Goddess. Finally, and most crucially, they transformed the simple Christian initiation of baptism into an elaborate Mystery, with all of the usual preparation and stage management necessary to produce an experience of insight, now that the activity of the possessing Spirit seems to have waned in direct proportion to the popularity of the faith.

The tone of Christian rhetoric changed dramatically. Dropping the harsh attacks on traditional religion and the Mysteries, Christian writers began to show how the Mysteries were part of God's plan to educate humanity and prepare it for the final great Mystery that Christianity offered. Every symbol, every insight was explained as leading up to the best Mystery of all. Constantine was praised by Christian leaders as a god on earth, as the second coming of the Messiah, as God's instrument to govern the whole world in a new era of peace. He built a fantastic new city in which he built temples to abstract principles that could embody many gods together. He filled the city with the finest representations of every god and goddess (though modern textbook perpetuate the Christian myth that Constantinople was a purely "Christian" city). It truly did seem like universal tolerance and harmony would prevail. But underneath, the conspiracy continued to eventually undermine and displace all rival spiritualities in the cause of the truth that Christianity alone possessed.

Constantine became more and more a pawn in the hands of a few unscrupulous Christian leaders. He was pushed into executing his young second wife and his eldest son on trumped up charges of an affair between them. Then his guilt over the deed was played upon to make him malleable in the hands of those who could promise him God's forgiveness. When revenues fell short, he was encouraged to plunder the few remaining temple treasuries untouched by Diocletian. His mother had become a full blown believer, and told her son that the Christian God had revealed to her several sites sacred to him. Constantine appropriated these sites, which were various sacred caves and groves around Jerusalem, and built churches upon them. His mother also "miraculously" discovered various sacred relics that became objects of worship, such as the cross on which Jesus was executed by the Romans three hundred years earlier. So, by a combination of adaptation and appropriation, Christianity made serious inroads into public life, displacing the traditional Mysteries.

In his old age, Constantine fell increasingly under the spell of a closed circle of the conspirators around him. He gave Christian leaders free use of the government courier system. He exempted them from certain taxes and civic responsibilities. In return, they fed his delusions of divinity and convinced him he could conquer the world if his armies were led by a rebuilt Ark of the Covenant. Only death forestalled the testing of this promise. In his will, Constantine treated the Empire itself with disdain, parceling it out among his three sons and two nephews as personal fiefdoms. The Christian sons immediately disposed of the non-Christian nephews, and began to undermine dramatically the tolerance their father had maintained. The harsher policy bred revolt in Rome, but the sole surviving son, Constantius, prevailed, and instituted even more severe measures. Sacrifice was prohibited and the major city temples closed to religious observances. Christian leaders were given increasing powers and privileges. They took over the public schools and used them to once again attack and ridicule the classic myths and spiritual practices of non-Christian culture. They even turned on each other, getting government help to drive into exile any Christian who refused to accept the one form of the faith they sanctioned (at this time, Arian Christianity).

A brief reprieve for traditional religion came with the revolt of Julian, sole survivor of the slaughtered non-Christian line of Constantine's dynasty. Taken from his home, he had been indoctrinated as a Christian and forced to prepare for the priesthood. Secretly, he studied the old ways, and was initiated into all the Mysteries. Given a military command in a desperate hour by the Emperor Constantius, he performed marvelously. But when word of his true spiritual inclinations leaked out, and he was recalled to Constantinople, his troops hoisted him on their shields and declared him Emperor, pledging their lives to displace the hated Constantius. Constantius conveniently died, leaving the way open to the energetic young conqueror. The whole Roman world, with the exception of the Christians, celebrated his ascent to power. He publicly declared his commitment to the old gods, and set about reorganizing and refunding their worship throughout the Empire. He introduced teacher testing, rooting out any teacher who used the classroom as a place to attack traditional culture. He delivered public speeches and published tracts comparing Christianity unfavorably to the Mysteries, and he wrote moving hymns reflecting his own spiritual devotion. He also recalled from exile all Christian leaders driven out by previous infighting, restoring them to their positions and property. He calculated, rightly, that Christians were their own worst enemy, and that they would fight and argue among themselves perpetually if no side could use government power against the others. A couple of the most obnoxious and abusive bishops were attacked in the streets by mobs and lynched in retaliation for the wanton acts of desecration they had perpetrated under the indulgent previous regime. When Julian came to Antioch to prepare an invasion of Persia, local Christians set fire to a major temple in the region, then complained bitterly when one of their churches was temporarily closed in retaliation. Julian gave permission and funds to the Jews to rebuild the Temple in Jerusalem. But Christian gangs attacked the construction works in the night, and torched the site. In time, Julian might have resorted to harsher measures and punishments to bring the Christians in line. But after only three short years, he had had enough taste of trying to govern hostile Christians to prefer the relative quiet of war. Not surprisingly, he was assassinated. Once again, Christian fiction steps in and tells us that with his dying words Julian recognized that the Christian God was destined to win. More reliable testimony informs us that he offered his own blood to the Unconquerable Sun, praying that the rest of his army would be spared and find their way home safely.

Julian was the last openly non-Christian Emperor of Rome. His death marked the beginning of the triumph of Christianity over the force of the Mysteries. With each successive administration, traditional religion was whittled away. At first, only overtly magical rituals were banned, and the Mysteries continued. But in the 380s the co-rulers Gratian and Theodosius brought a new level of fanaticism to an Empire that could ill afford it. They refused to take the oath as Pontifex Maximus, by which they were bound to manage and protect all religious institutions in the Empire. They removed the altar of victory from the Roman senate house. They stripped Jews and Manichaeans of their legal rights, confiscated their property, and drew up long lists of outlawed varieties of Christianity itself, driving thousands from the cities. This only served their need for resources by which to support the form of faith they chose to sanction, (Catholic/Orthodox Christianity), which up until now had been decidedly in the minority. They closed all the temples, and appropriated all temple funds. The Mysteries were suspended. Finally, they drove traditional religion out of public life altogether and proposed, although the means were not at their disposal, to root it even out of the home.

Non-conformist Christians and traditionalists formed an odd alliance that disposed of Gratian and freed Rome temporarily from this oppressive regime. Theodosius set out to crush the revolt and, not trusting Roman troops in this fight, hired a mercenary army of Goths. The opposing armies met at Frigidus in northern Italy, the standards of Jupiter against the standards of Christ. For two days the future of the West hung in the balance. In the end, the hastily gathered Roman forces could not match the tough mercenaries of Theodosius.

For the next century and a half, Christianity dug ever deeper into the native soil. Temples were systematically confiscated and converted into churches. Legends were created of how the local "demon" was driven out by the power of a priest or monk. Sacred trees were cut down, sacred springs sealed or polluted. A mob of monks attacked the great Museon in Alexandria, pulling down the statue of Serapis who oversaw the four thousand year old Egyptian Mysteries, and burning its Library to the ground. Later Christian historians fabricated contradictory stories of the Library being burned by Julius Caesar four hundred years earlier, or by the Muslims three hundred years later, to cover up responsibility in this devastating loss of ancient wisdom. Christianity had entered a period of all-out assault on traditional religion and the Mysteries. Having seized control of the cities, they labeled all traditionalists "pagans" or country-folk. The cultured classes willingly gave up the cities for life in the country where they could practice their traditional religion in peace, and closer to the nature that embodied it. As a result, civic life all but ceased. The cities became ghost towns where only churches and their dependents remained. Imperial legislation was ignored and unenforced in most rural areas. Though the Mysteries were a thing of the past, the memory of them and the worldview they offered was preserved in the resistance literature of the Fifth and Sixth centuries, which passed itself off as commentaries on the classics or antiquarian studies.

The victory of Christianity was the death of the Roman world. The disaffected country landholders welcomed Gothic and German invaders and formed new nations with them. The Empire struck back under Justinian in the mid-Fifth century. He recaptured Rome and Carthage. He closed the university in Athens, the last non-Christian center of learning. He shut down the last large operating temple, that of Isis at Philae at the border with Nubia. He burned whole villages with their inhabitants to the ground because they held on to "paganism" or some variety of Christianity he refused to recognize. On paper, he seemed to reconstitute the Empire of old on a new Christian footing. But his actions only bred hatred and resistance. The Egyptian and Syrian Christians rejected his interpretation of Christianity, while the countryside seethed with rebellion. Within a century of his death, the much more tolerant Muslims had seized control of the Middle East, greeted by jubilant crowds as liberators, an ironic scenario from the contemporary Western perspective. The deeply embedded thinking of the Mysteries found new clothing in esoteric teachings of the Monophysite Christians, and in the practices of the Islamic Sufis. European traditionalists also hung on, sometimes wrapping beliefs and practices in Christian garb, other times celebrating them in all their raw "paganism." One by one, Christianity won control of the ruling classes of the new European nations, but the imposition of the faith on the common people varied with the whim of individual rulers. Only in the Twelfth century did Catholicism start to make serious inroads into rural life in Europe, and only with puritanical Protestantism and the age of witch-burning did Christianity seal the tomb of the last remnants of the old religion.

But the Mysteries in their original form were long since silenced. Only echoes in fragmented ritual, songs, and folk tales carried hints of long-forgotten views. The full Mysteries had fallen victim to the holocaust that swept over traditional religion between the late Fourth and early Seventh centuries, the culmination of a deliberate and relentless campaign to rid society as much as possible of pre-Christian spirituality.

Though this destruction appeared successful *for a time,* no final victory can be declared, as so many men of the mind have noted, including the Mage Israel Regardie who said, "We are now seeing the death throws of Christianity...its final death squeeze on Western Consciousness." According to Dr. Hyatt he said this a few years before his death in 1985, and the sales of books focusing both on the ancient mysteries and alternative religious experience have more than tripled. In the final analysis there can be no holocaust of the human mind.

ON CYMBALS

QUESTION REALITY

BY MOBIUSFRAME

Before we begin our discussion of the reality defining properties of questions, let us consider some definitions:

Norm: A standard social model or pattern regarded as acceptable; an average of dominant memes in a given social group, usually accepted without analysis or question. Consider the circumcision of male infants as a social "norm."

Normative: Conforming to the established (dogmatic) language usage of educated speakers in a given society. Synonym = prescriptive. Consider that if the police ask you a question, regardless of its absurdity, you must answer. "Yes or no, did you use a knife to kill your neighbor?" This is an ill-formed question; it presupposes that you killed your neighbor.

Prescriptive: Based on or prescribing a norm or standard (non-observable suppositions); giving directives or rules: Art & fashion, law, mores, common sense.

Presupposition: Reasoning that involves the formation of conclusions from incomplete evidence.

Empiric: Regarding an objective collection of data points (evidence) for the synthesis of suppositions.

Empirical: Derived from observation and experiment rather than theory; capable of being tested (falsified or verified) by experiment or observation. Synonym = data-based. Antonym = theoretical.

Descriptive: Concerned with phenomena at a given moment, without consideration of historical antecedent or norms: based on observed phenomena.

Moral (metaphysical) paradigm	Scientific paradigm
Normative Definitions	Empirical Definitions
Prescriptive Grammar	Descriptive Grammar
"Ought to/Should"	"Is"
Valuation	Fact
Subjective	Objective
Presuppositions likely	No presupposition

Even a cursory understanding of linguistics and hypnosis reveals that the language used by speakers in communicating not only describes their reality, but also forms and constructs their "perceived" reality. Thus, the words and sentence structures with which one speaks and thinks creates and manifests his reality. Language communicates information (descriptive/empirical function), and it also coordinates and directs behaviors by stirring feelings like wellness, guilt, pride, and shame (prescriptive/normative function).

In the case of hypnosis, my reality, as expressed by the words I use, may alter your reality if you accept the words and phrases I speak to you. Accepting the words of a statement or question need not occur consciously, and in fact, it rarely does. Hopefully, the gentle reader already has a decent level of skill in detecting and rejecting obviously false, or ill formed statements such as: "The earth is flat."[False, see NASA photographs of earth] or "Jesus is my lord and savior." [Ill-formed, cannot be tested empirically].

I find it relatively simple to detect the ill-formed-ness of a statement. However, an ill-formed question, especially if posed by someone that you consider an authority figure, or if posed in a violent or accusatory manner, may prove more difficult to detect. Adrenaline mercilessly slays analytical and cognitive ability, sending one quickly to the irrational animal mind where ill-formed language is likely to be accepted wholesale. Without analysis and rational cognition, ill-formed questions and statements are accepted and internalized, thereby forming ones reality without detection. This is a form of hypnosis.

The Question Game: The Inquisition.

"A question as a question is simply a question; however, for most monkeys a question has tension and freezes the brain......"

— Dr. Hyatt

Mother/father/god/cop/judge/priest asks a question, and the child/parishioner/heretic/infidel/criminal answers. The first question to ask is: Is the question answerable? Are all the terms in the question capable of some empirical (i.e., non-normative) definition? Whoever asks this type of moral question expressed in normative grammar is playing a "one up game" in which they presuppose themselves as the deity (moral authority). A whole host of other presuppositions may be present in the language structure of the question, and upon answering the question, the child/parishioner/heretic/infidel/criminal accepts the presuppositions as true, and validates the irrational stance of the inquisitor. You must learn to avoid switching over to fight-or-flight response, and you must learn to spot poorly formed questions.

Avoid Chemical Brain Freeze

Some people can ask questions of you and you simply answer. Other people (e.g., spouse, police, parent, priest, combatant, etc.) may ask a question and instantly send you into a "chemical brain freeze," also known as fight-or-flight. The major key in avoiding brain freeze is to remain calm and detached, which can be nearly impossible in some circumstances. However, like all good personality change, it will take effort, time & patience. Train yourself to make your initial response to any question calm and patient. Your first response to any question then should be the following:

1. Take three deep breaths, hold each breath for a few seconds, and then gently release. The inquisitor will likely become impatient and fidgety, or may even become more agitated. Do not allow this to affect you. You will answer the question if and when you choose. Focus on the feeling of the breaths.

2. Smile: This will send signals to you brain that relax you and enhance cognition. Fake it if necessary. It should feel and look genuine — avoid the "devil's grimace."

3. Detach: Force yourself to stop experiencing this as a threat. This will require effort and work on your part.

4. Analyze: If you have successfully avoided the Sympathetic Nervous System response (fight-or-flight = adrenaline), you are ready to move on to **analysis.**

Analyze these 3 points when considering a question put to you:

a. What physical signals does the inquisitor exhibit?

Pupils dilated means the target is adrenalized and ready for battle.

Pointing fingers, shrugged shoulders, or any extreme gesticulation signals that an emotional response is occurring (emotions don't mix with calm cool analysis). Also note facial contortion like a furrowed brow or a frown.

Pulse rate and blood pressure often takes a moderate level of skill to discern, but you can easily notice if veins are bulging on the side of the head/face or neck (high blood pressure), and the pulse can often be seen in the carotid artery alongside the neck, especially if the target is aroused.

Flared nostrils and rapid, shallow breathing are also signs of emotional arousal/distress.

b. What, if any, are the presuppositions of the question? Presupposition is probably the most common hypnotic technique used in manipulative language. Study presuppositions. Below are a few basic examples of presupposition. See if you can spot the presupposed ideations:

> (1) How often do you beat your wife?

> (2) When will you call me?

> (3) How often do you use drugs?

c. Are the terms of the question definable empirically?

Do you love me? This cannot be tested empirically. There is no way to measure or observe love.

"Have you accepted the Lord Jesus Christ as your savior?" Same as above, since there is no way to prove or disprove.

"Why are you like this?" "This" is a vague pronoun, and could mean anything.

"Do you believe in American values and the verity of justice?" This question essentially means nothing, but it looks great on paper.

Keep in mind that many people will ask questions only to demonstrate their authoritative knowledge of a subject area. These people are severe time wasters, loaded with hair-splitting questions so they may show off their metapuke superiority. If you suspect this may be the case, respond to the questions with questions. Turn the haughty self-aggrandizing rubbish back on the inquisitor. You might ask them, "What makes you think you've asked a real question? What do you want? Are you trying to help? And if so, what? What will you decide when you get an answer?" Remember, oftentimes the purpose of questions is to coerce you into accepting the inquisitor as a judge and someone with the right to make a moral pronouncement. Try to determine the hidden metaphysical agenda of these idiots, and then question it.

Establishing Rapport with the Target

If you want to get along with someone, learn when to ask the right questions. The right question at the right time shows interest. The wrong question at the wrong time will be perceived as an attack! A question always asks something of the target. At the very least, a question is the act of asking for a response from the target. Thus, a question is a confrontation of wills. To get along with someone, your will must appear to be identical to, or at least parallel to, the will of the target.

Consider the beauty you'd like to take home tonight. Any good hunter knows that patience and the ability to plan for the future will yield the best results. If her will is to avoid you at all costs, you will establish rapport more quickly if it appears that you wish to avoid *her* at all costs. Otherwise, you just bother her. Likewise, consider that interview for the job you really want. You are a staunch conservative, while the big boss is a hardcore liberal. If you want to have a great conversation and a new job, you will appear liberal as well. This doesn't mean you agree with everything the target says; rather, a little engagement will make you appear lively. However, the target's ego must be made to feel special while in your presence. Thus, your presence will be desired.

Along with the right questions, mimicking the target's posture, mannerisms, and tone of voice, at least initially, establishes rapport (leading). Then, as you alter your mirroring of them, they will mimic you (pacing). All this must be done very slowly and with greatest patience and ease. Also, note the output phraseology of the target. If it is speaking about visual data, and using visual statements, respond in kind. The same applies to auditory and kinesthetic statements as shown below:

• Visual target output: "I look forward to brightening up our company's reputation. I hope you're the man for the job."

Practitioner responds in visual phraseology: "Yes sir, I see things your way, and with your visionary guidance, I'm confident that I can shed light on the problem areas."

• Audio target output: "I've heard a lot of good things about you. Sounds like you may be the man to help us regain our fast-paced rhythm in the markets."

Practitioner responds in auditory phraseology: "Yes sir, I hear the sincerity in your voice, and with your words of guidance, I'm confident that I can make the goals of this company ring true."

• Kinesthetic target output: "I feel that we need a confident man to get a handle on some of the burning issues around here. I have a good feeling about you, and it seems that you may be the man to help us regain our footing in the markets."

Practitioner responds in kinesthetic phraseology: "Yes sir, I've always felt that this company is the best in the market. I feel very excited about joining the team and getting my feet wet. I'm confident that I can actualize the goals of this company."

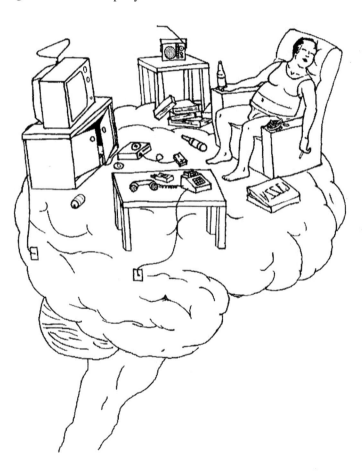

On Drums

The Terrible 3s
A Sail on the Titanic[1]

by Christopher S. Hyatt, Ph.D.

What do we know of ourselves? At best, a metaphor.

> — C.S. Hyatt, Ph.D.

I have never seen a triangle that can stand on two legs.

> — C.S. Hyatt, Ph.D.

A metaphor: "A figure of speech in which a word or phrase that ordinarily designates one thing is used to designate another, thus making an implicit comparison, as in 'a sea of troubles.'"

The trip on the Titanic ended in disaster. And so have all theories of personality......

Metaphors always break down, but they do convey a message.

Labels are even worse as they sooner or later become infected with the zombie virus known as morality — a weak man's tonic.

In today's world, personality will best be understood by complex mathematics and neuroscience coupled with complex computer modeling.

In my view, however, no matter how much we know and how precise we become there will always be a wild card. Why? Because with proper use the brain can drastically change and each change begins to interact with every other change and sooner or later we reach escape velocity and a new monster is born. So enjoy the journey while you can......

---

[1] Cheap Tickets

It's Unsinkable

Self 1: The Bio-Self (**BS**)......automatic existential self......everyone has one—much like a reptile—fully reactive to changing chemical and physical conditions......a simple survival tool. Assuming you are breathing, no matter how mad you are, you have this self.

Self 2: The Ego-Self (**ES**)......semi-automatic, interactive, semi-thinking self......most everyone has one to one degree or another—much like an advanced "ape."

Intelligent action limited, emotional reaction, some mild forms of tense-less self-consciousness, mostly a function of memory......capable of some intentional action, primarily reactive in nature......confuses needs and wants with love......capable of some enjoyment, senselessly suffers over itself......can be objective about things but not about self. Has no real sense of itself, deluded by language, infected with beliefs. A sorrowful creature.

Self 3: The Transcendent-Self (TS)......a self artificially created through self-work and intense effort......very few have one—similar to the imaginary idea of a god......capable of real choice, active, highly intentional action......capable of love and being loved, capable of being objective about self—special abilities......high energy, low tension.

Where To Place Your BET?

Step one: accept you are a bio-chemical machine and understand intellectually what that means *in detail*.

Step two: identify the qualities and reactions of the machine by using one's false sense of self-consciousness and the super-ego.

Step three: use the reactions of the machine to build the TS.

Step four: identify the techniques required.

Step five: practice every day.

Step six: 00.

They First Met On The Promenade Deck

The Bio-Self and the Ego-Self are continually interacting with each other, creating an almost never-ending train of illusions and delusions...... In the human the ego-self has the use of language which disguises the bio-self and ego-self reactions...... With language, the human turns these automated reactions into actions as if it were a fully conscious willful being...... This ideal is based on a vague sense of the " higher" self...... On occasion, many humans will have experiences (so-called "peak experiences") which the ego attributes to this illusory "higher" self......which in fact doesn't exist in substance, but only as an ideal...... These "peak experiences" are a result of chemicals, stress factors, athletics and numerous other events, *but they are not a self.*

Four Egos Are Not Enough

The Ego-Self has four parts.

First is the primal part, directly connected with the bio-brain...... This is the (beast), the sado-masochist, the crazy one, a dark shadow, etc.

The next part is the social-cultural-interpersonal piece, the so-called self-concept or self-esteem — with occasional tense self-consciousness.

Next is a cognitive problem-solving part and, like an engorged appendix, contains the small possibility to develop the TS......

This part — and threads from the first, second, and third pieces — form to make what is called the superego — the fourth part......

This part, the judge, watches and often hates the previous three parts......

Here is the kicker: the judge — the superego — is the root from which the TS can develop — ironic, but true...... A happy reptile or ape would never think to develop a TS.

It is from pain and conflict that the possibility arises, so the human and not the dog is the candidate....... It is only the "awareness" of suffering and death that make this possible.

As an interesting example, let us look at the Buddha — What led him to seek enlightenment? The suffering and death he saw and then his comparison to his life — followed by what Freud or the Christians might call — guilt...... Both factors, the realization of suffering and the guilt he felt over not experiencing it...... He was, after all, a blind, happy ape rolling around in the green and having fun...... That was his garden of Eden, but he created his own fall — unlike the Jew-Christian-Muslim...... Hence, for Buddha, his salvation was not vicarious; rather, through his own hard-won efforts......he "created" the fall, and finds his own salvation......

Today this is rarely possible...... Look at how easy it is to be a dumb monkey......

49

Look at the Jesus story: his suffering on the cross leads to the final transcendence of his ego and body-self. Do you buy this? But again, look at the dual aspects of suffering and transcendence in this story.

The suffering of the Jewish people, the Arabs, the Germans, the Chinese, the Russians and on and on we go, suffering and transcendence; however, no TS develops—except in the case of Buddha.

The base of all change, both individually and collectively, is suffering, pain and dissatisfaction; however, unlike the beauty of the lotus flower with its roots in the mud, mankind simply changes the label......and continues to suffer.

To sum up: the suffering we cause ourselves and each other has greater value than we know—for a few men—one at a time, by their own efforts—can turn this form of human stupidity into a real self, far beyond the limitations set by nature.

On Violins

Entrance Piece

by Joseph Matheny

You are expecting an ending here, I just know it. Instead, I am going to propose an entrance. What I mean by this is, this would be an ending, if we were to so declare it but instead, we propose that you make it an entrance to a new beginning. You've heard the old hackneyed phrase, "There are no endings, only beginnings" or some form thereof. However, at the risk of sounding clichéd, this is your golden opportunity to walk away. Just put the book down and walk away. <insert voice through megaphone here>: "Walk away from the book…"

STILL HERE? OK, I GUESS I CAN UNDERSTAND THAT.

Here's the score: What you do with the information that you absorbed from the preceding chapters is now yours to do with as you wish. What THEY don't tell you is that the final door (the ending Hey) in the Tetragrammaton is an exit. The formula is a finger pointing (pointing the way in), a door (you open it and enter willingly), a fish hook (you could get hung up on the barb and stay here, becoming middle management), and a final Hey (the fucking door out of the system). Now you know.

STILL HERE? OK, NOW I'M BECOMING A LITTLE SUSPICIOUS OF YOU…

Let me try to make this perfectly clear. This is the part where you expect me to get up on a soapbox and make a summation. I refuse to do it. Thesis and antithesis can be drawn from the preceding chapters but the synthesis is up to you. I'm not going to do your work for you, you lazy bastard! Nor am I going to rob you of that magical aha! experience that comes when you make your own synthesis. It's not a complete imprint unless you do it yourself. Now get to it!

There are no answers, only choices. If you bought this book looking for an answer of some sort, I suggest you rip the pages out now and use them as toilet paper. There's your answer. If, on the other hand, you view this chapter, not as an exit, not as a final statement, but rather as an entrance to the Garden of Forked Paths, you have probably ended up in a place where you belong. At least there's hope for you yet.

Mutate and take over the world? Nah. Been said, been tried and really, what's the point? Mutate and ignore the world? That's been tried, too. Unfortunately, the world (THEM) has a habit of barging into your dream-time village and making you pay attention to it, no matter how diligently you try to ignore it (THEM). What is one to do then? Maybe, mutate and LIVE? Now there's a palatable proposition. Mmmmmmmmm! One could even imagine that going well with Fava beans.

It can be said that life is a game. If that is true, who's controlling your avatar? Who wrote the code? What's the underlying language? There I go again, leaving you with questions rather than supplying you with convenient answers. I am so evil. <insert-menacing laugh—add moderate echo effect> Have you noticed that we've recommended other books to read as you've moved through this little grimoire of pure evil? Will you read them? Are we attempting to brainwash you or entrain you into a different way of thinking? Do you feel different after reading the preceding chapters? Do you feel like a lab rat? My, but you are paranoid aren't you? Don't be so narcissistic.

I'm so selfless that I'm not only not writing for or to you, I am not even writing for or to myself. That's how selfless and Ghandi-like I am. What a guy, huh? Ok, I'll be up front and blunt for a second. I could truly give a shit what you think. How's that for blunt. Now, to take it one step further, you should truly give a shit what I think as well. In fact, you should rip this book up and use it as kindling starter in your fireplace. If you don't have a fireplace, then start a fire on your living room floor. Do something fer cripes sake. Speaking of doing something…

When viewing the sedentary lifestyle of TV and bad beer that so many subscribe to these days, the term "get a life" takes on a whole new meaning. What? You missed the final episode of *Friends*? Pshaw! You captured it on Tivo. You can now put in lot's of overtime since you're doing three people's jobs now, and be paid for regular time, since you should just be grateful to even HAVE a job, you miserable little worm, and you can still have something to share in common at the water cooler, thanks to your Tivo. Moooooooooo!

The wonders of technology never cease! Ok, pull back for a minute. Think about all the little munchkins gathered around the warm glow of the electric campfire every night. Prime Time. All watching the same things (hearing the same campfire stories) all sunken into their easy chairs and couches. All plugged into the...no, I'm not gonna say it. It's been overused and besides, parts two and three sucked. Anyway, you get my drift. Walk down your street at night, around TV Prime Time and look at all those windows glowing blue gray. What does this remind you of? Ever been to a farm and seen how they fatten veal? Ever studied how Kobe beef is raised? Now the question (always questions): What are you being fattened up for? Or more precisely, as food for what or whom?

Look into the effects of light pulsation upon the human brain. Did you know that TV works on a scan method; i.e., the screen is rapidly refreshed at a rate of 60 kHz? Most computer monitors come preset to this frequency as well. In other words, it is flashing at you in rapid light pulses. Do you really think this doesn't affect your brain state? How much TV have you watched in your lifetime? Jeebus! That much?

We have about 150,000 hours of living to expend between the ages of one and 18.

We sleep about 50,000 hours of this time, and we dream about two hours of the eight we sleep each night. Sleeping and dreaming appear to be positively related to the development and maintenance of the long term memories that emerge out of daytime activities, because they allow our brain to eliminate the interference of external sensory/motor activity while it physically adds to, edits, and erases the neural network synaptic connections that create long-term memories.

We spend about 65,000 of our 100,000 waking hours involved in solitary activities, and in direct informal relationships with family and friends, and these activities play a major role in the development and maintenance of important personal memories.

We spend about 35,000 of our waking hours with our larger culture in formal and informal metaphoric/symbolic activities—about 12,000 hours in school, and about twice that much with various forms of mass media (e.g., TV, computers, films, music, sports, non-school print media, churches, museums). Mass media and school thus play major roles in the development and maintenance of important culture memories.

So on an average developmental day between the ages of 1–18, a young person sleeps 8 hours, spends 10 waking hours with self, family, and friends, 4 with mass media—and only 2 hours in school.

People tend now to spend much time/energy on such electronic media as video games, TV, and computers—at the expense of non-electronic media and socialization (although new forms of socialization are evolving around TV-watching and video-game-playing).

The attentional demands of electronic media range from rapt (video games) to passive (much TV), but this is the first generation to directly interact with and alter the content on the screen and the conversation on the radio. Screenagers emotionally understand electronic media in ways that adults don't—as a viral replicating cultural reality, instead of as a mere communicator of events. For example, portable cameras have helped to shift TV's content from dramatic depiction's to live theater, extended (and often endlessly repeated and discussed) live coverage of such breaking events as wars, accidents, trials, sports, and talk-show arguments. What occurs anywhere is immediately available everywhere. Our world has truly become a gossipy global village, where everyone knows everyone else's business.

Emotion drives attention, which drives learning, memory, and behavior, so mass media often insert strong primal emotional elements into their programming to increase attention. Since violence and sexuality in media trigger primal emotions, most young people confront thousands of violent acts and heavy doses of sexuality during their childhood media interactions. This comes at the expense, alas, of other more positive and normative experiences with human behaviors and interactions. Mass media tend to show us how to be sexy not sexual, and powerful not peaceful.

Commercial sponsorship in mass media has led to a distorted presentation of important cultural and consumer-related issues. For example, TV commercials tend to be very short, superficial, and factually biased. Further, computer programs and TV editing techniques tend to compress, extend, and distort normal time/space relationships, a critically important element in the creation and use of effective long-term memories.

1. A relatively slow, analytic, reflective system (thalamus-hippocampus-cortex circuitry) explores the more objective factual elements of a situation, compares them with related declarative memories, and then responds. It's best suited to non-threatening situations that don't require an instant response—life's little challenges. It often functions through storytelling forms and sequences, and so is tied heavily to our language and classification capabilities. User-friendly computer programs and non-frantic TV programming tend to use this rational system.

2. A fast conceptual, reflexive system (thalamus-amygdala-cerebellum circuitry) identifies the fearful and survival elements in a situation, and quickly activates automatic response patterns (procedural memory) if survival seems problematic.

The fast system developed through natural selection to respond to imminent predatory danger and fleeting feeding and mating opportunities. It thus focuses on any loud/looming/contrasting/moving/obnoxious/attractive elements that might signal potential danger, food, and/or mates.

The system thus enhances survival, but its rapid superficial analysis often leads us to respond fearfully, impulsively, and inappropriately to situations that didn't require an immediate response (regrets and apologies often follow). Stereotyping and prejudice are but two of the prices we humans pay for this powerful survival system. Worse, fear can strengthen the emotional and weaken the factual memories of an event. Consequently, we become fearful of something, but we're not sure why, so the experience has taught us little that's consciously useful.

People often use mass media to exploit this system by stressing elements that trigger rapid irrational fear-responses. Politicians demonize opponents; sales pitches demand an immediate response; zealots focus on fear of groups who differ from their definition of acceptable.

The fast pacing of TV and video game programming, and their focus on bizarre/violent/sexual elements also trigger this system. If the audience perceives these elements and the resulting visceral responses as the real-world norm, the electronic media must continually escalate the violent/sexual/bizarre behavior to trigger the fast system. Rational thought development would thus suffer. We can see this escalation in mass media.

Conversely, if a person perceives these electronic-world elements as an aberration, and not normative of the real world, such electronic experiences could often actually help to develop rational thought and appropriate response. Those who will understand the normative center of a phenomenon must also know about its outer reaches—and mass media provide a useful metaphoric format for observing the outer reaches of something without actually experiencing it (such as how to escape from a dangerous situation one might confront)[2]

WE NOW INTERRUPT OUR REGULARLY SCHEDULED PROGRAM TO BRING YOU THIS SPECIAL ANNOUNCEMENT

Effects on Sensory Development

Children who are actively playing will have more opportunity to develop their senses than children passively viewing. By its very nature, TV is an impoverished sensory environment. In a recent study comparing TV viewing with laboratory simulated sensory deprivation, researchers found that 96 hours of laboratory-induced sensory deprivation produced the same effects on the person as only a few minutes of TV viewing. Normal sensory experience is vital to maintaining a balanced state of mind and body.

---

[2] *The Effects of Electronic Media On A Developing Brain,* Robert Sylwester, University of Oregon.

Sight

While viewing, the eyes are practically motionless and "defocused" in order to take in the whole screen. Constant movement is required for healthy eye development. Visual exploration is a prerequisite of seeing, and necessary for developing a sense of depth and perspective. The two-dimensional screen does not facilitate such development The sense of sight is maturing through age 12. Excessive TV viewing, one of the most passive visual activities, can seriously impair a child's observational skills. Viewing affects not only eye mechanics, but also the ability to focus and pay attention.

Hearing

Since TV is more visual than auditory, children's sense of hearing is not being fully exercised. Active listening is a skill that needs to be developed. Children need practice in processing auditory stimulation, making their own mental pictures in response to what they hear. Also, when TV is constantly on, the sense of hearing may be dulled by the persistent background noise.

Sense of Wonder

The subtle rhythms and patterns of life's wonders which can only be appreciated through patient observation and experience will hold little interest for a child given a steady diet of TV. The fast paced, action-packed, high drama which is programmed to keep viewers tuned in does not accurately represent the natural world, yet it is what children come to expect. Real experiences, therefore, can't compete with TV and the child's sense of wonder is dulled.

Effects on Health

Because of the activities it displaces, TV viewing certainly impacts motor coordination, balance, and general level of fitness. Yet there are other, perhaps less obvious, effects.

Radiation and Artificial Light

Early research on radiation has led to a substantial reduction in the amount of X-rays being emitted. Little experimental evidence exists on the effects of artificial light on people; further research is needed before conclusions can be made. In the meantime, children should be nourished as much as possible by natural light, and not "overdosed" with artificial TV light.

Obesity

Elevated cholesterol and obesity are two of the most prevalent nutritional diseases among U.S. children today. TV viewing has been found to be associated with both of these conditions. Likewise, viewing correlates significantly with between-meal snacking, consumption of advertised foods, and attempts to influence mothers' food purchases.

Sleep Deprivation

Many studies indicate that children are staying up late to watch TV. One reported that children as young as eight were still watching TV at 11:30 pm on school nights. Teachers comment that children are too tired and irritable to work well after late night viewing. Sleep is a physical necessity, required to build up the growing organism. It is also a psychological necessity, the prerequisite for dreaming. Yet dreams after TV viewing may be disturbed, with vivid TV images resurfacing and causing nightmares.

Effects on Cognitive and Intellectual Development

Numerous child development and educational experts express great concern with television's numbing effect on children's brains. Many reports suggest that children's minds are not developing the way they should, and this is attributed in large measure to excessive TV viewing.

Language Acquisition

In the early years, when the brain is so malleable and sensitive, TV viewing prolongs the dominance of right brain functions which induce a trance-like state. When viewed for more than 20 hours per week, TV can seriously inhibit the development of verbal-logical, left-brain functions. The patterning that the brain needs for language development is hindered by viewing during this language-sensitive period of infancy, and it may be more difficult to acquire speech later on. Studies document that general word knowledge and vocabulary are not affected either positively or negatively by TV, but that creative verbal fluency is lower for children who watch TV more because it does not offer time for interactive play and conversation.

Reading Skills

There are more videotape stores than book stores in the U.S. today. A great many studies have documented declining literacy rates over the last thirty years. TV viewing is an easier and preferred activity compared to the challenge of book reading, especially for children who have not yet developed fluent reading skills. TV requires little concentration, defocuses the mind, offers electronically produced images, and encourages passivity, while reading necessitates concentration, thought, focusing, and the ability to visualize. Television trains short attention spans, while reading trains long attention spans. Studies suggest that light viewers learn to read more easily than heavy viewers. Research into brain wave patterns confirm these differences. Studies of both children's and adults' brain wave patterns while viewing TV confirm that brain activity switches from beta (indicating alert and conscious attention) to alpha waves within thirty seconds of turning the set on. Greatly increased alpha waves resulted regardless of whether children were interested in the program or not. The electrical responses of the brain while viewing resemble those which do not normally occur when the eyes are open.

Effects on Creativity and Imagination

Boredom is the empty space necessary for creativity. With TV filling a child's leisure moments, the necessary void is never experienced. Additionally, the child's play is often restricted to forms prescribed by adult programmers whose primary objective is to sell toys. With pre-determined themes and ready-made playthings, little is left to the imagination.

Furthermore, when children are bombarded with TV images, their own ability to form imaginative pictures becomes severely impaired. This process of generating internal pictures is critical to the development of dendrites and neural connectors which lay the foundation for intelligence and creativity. Studies which have investigated how TV viewing affects performance in creative problem-solving suggest that excessive viewing may lead to decreased attention, persistence, and tolerance. The displacement of problem-solving opportunities also results in a more limited repertoire of creative solutions.

Effects on Social Development

Television is not a substitute for meeting and interacting with real people in real situations. A child cannot develop a sense of self in the absence of contact with others. While viewing, a child is not gaining practice in relating to others, and in constructive interpersonal problem-solving. Furthermore, most TV problems are framed in oversimplified, black-white thinking and resolved, often violently, in one hour (less commercial breaks).

Findings have consistently demonstrated that violence on TV correlates with subsequent aggressive behavior. Recent evidence from an extensive longitudinal study carried out in four different countries suggests there is a sensitive period that begins before age eight when children are especially susceptible to the effects of violence shown on TV.

Effects on Perceptions of Reality

Heavy TV viewers develop a distorted sense of reality. Most notable may be an exaggerated perception of the prevalence of violence in society, which comes from an over-representation of violent acts in programs. (The frequency of violence in children's programs is six times greater than that of adults').[3]

PUT THIS BOOK DOWN AND TAKE THAT WALK BEFORE YOU READ ANOTHER WORD. NO, REALLY.

I see that you're back. Do you always do what your told? Heh-heh-heh! You are making me repeat myself and that is pissing me off.

Ok, I'm going to stop fucking with you now. If you've endured until now, you deserve this. I'm going to tell you the real secrets. It's what you've been waiting for, right? Good doggy. You followed the trail this far. Now comes the money shot.

Secret number one... Wait, I have a few more things to say before I get to that. I'm getting there, hang on. I want to talk about video games and on-line games for a minute.

Tripping the Photon Phantastic

Immersive gaming is in the tradition of psychonautic and cybernautic exploration. But while its connections to the supermind and cyberpunk are fairly clear, does the gaming experience really compare in intensity of experience or effect to what is suggested as the first historical coun-

---

[3] *Study Links Aggressive Adults, TV Viewing*, Malcolm Ritter

terpart, the radical reality-estrangement of taking psychedelic drugs? Consider a typical trip report: "It was as if my room were reduced to a 2-dimensional picture which was subsequently torn to confetti and thrown into a blender. My head was attached to R's arm. My foot is sticking out of the wall, next to a book which had somehow fused with my alarm clock. All concept of space, time, and direction are scrambled. 'I' is not even a vaguely remembered concept. Ultimate chaos. Ultimate fear." Certainly, this reaction is more severe than a typical gamer's as I have described it above. Yet, the estrangement from customary consciousness and social relations that immersive gaming provides has, I believe, a few potential advantages over psychedelic drugs and the earlier cyberpunk movement in generating lasting change in subjectivity.

First, in terms of attracting new explorers, games can provide a much less frightening and more seductively pleasant path than psychedelic drugs. With gaming, there is not only less of a perceived physical risk, and therefore less of an impeding fear factor, but also less intention required on the part of the participant. Many non-evolutionary-minded players, ostensibly in search of simple entertainment, find themselves inadvertently implicated in and motivated by the opportunity for new modes of human being.

This increased availability of prospective participants is compounded by the opportunity for extended simultaneous exploration among immersive gamers. Although web sites such as lyceaum.org and thedrugsindex.org have taken advantage of digital technology to allow for greater distribution of knowledge on where to obtain, how to prepare, or how to endure psychedelic drugs, these forums do not yet orchestrate real-time communities of simultaneous exploration. Immersive gaming, on the other hand, provides numerous opportunities for massively multi-player simultaneous gaming, connecting thousands of players in live online and offline communities. To this extent, immersive gaming has succeeded in engineering huge and widely distributed networks of experience, whereas psychonauts have been limited to comparatively local exploration. This distribution is important not only for potential outreach, but also for creating the large-scale feedback systems and contextual reinforcement necessary for sustained and group-directed change. It also, through sheer magnitude of mind share, exponentially heightens the potential subjective multiplicity.

Another potential strength of immersive gaming as an agent for change is the absence of a "coming down" factor. With psychedelic drugs, users return from a totally alternate reality to an everyday reality that looks, sounds, and feels like the pre-trip world. Things in this "real world" exist in contrast to the experience of the trip. The user may feel irrevocably changed, perhaps mentally or spiritually, by the experience, but the everyday world itself has not been substantially altered. In a Web document entitled "Psychedelic Experience F.A.Q", first-time users are advised of numerous "post-effects" that accompany psychedelic experimentation, including "disorientation" and "insights"; they are assured, however, that "All the following effects share one characteristic: their frequency and/or intensity decreases with time. Fully returning to baseline usually takes around one month, although most of these disappear entirely within a week." For immersive gamers, on the other hand, the everyday world is so much a part of the alternate reality they experience, the player never "comes down" from the experience. The game world is not set in contrast to everyday life, so "post-effects" persist indefinitely in non-game life.[4]

---

[4] *"This Is Not a Game": Collective Subjectivity and Immersive Entertainment* Jane McGonigal. More info: http://joseph.matheny.com/ARG.html

Rhetorical Analysis as Methodology

Although traditionally focused on immediate verbal symbols, particularly oral and written, rhetorical perspective can be used to analyze a variety of forms, including other symbolic modes (such as music or dance), and communication designed to transcend time and context. An expanded definition of rhetoric is expressed as "the management of symbols in order to coordinate social action." (Hauser, 1986) Popular discourse also refers to the product of this management as "rhetoric." Rhetorical analysis stresses the interpretation of artifacts from a rhetorical perspective, and by focusing on the interpretation of the artifact, distances itself from questions of authorial intent. Feminist rhetorician Susan Foss also extends the scope of rhetorical expression to include non-combative persuasion (persuasion that does not intend to change the position of the audience, but to gain acceptance for the position of the speaker).

Why This Approach?

Games offer a unique format in which the player/audience has some opportunity to control and configure their experience. Interactive game players thrive on a sense of agency—a desire to see the results of their interactions. This desire is amplified in online games, which offer players the opportunity to communicate with a wide audience.

ARE YOU GETTING IT YET?

OK, NOW TO THOSE SECRETS.

Secret number one…oh, shit. I'm over my word count. Sorry, we'll have to get to those secrets another time. In the meantime, I'll be downloading a pirate version of *Natural Born Killers* on Kazaa lite. A man's gotta have his culture, after all.

THE BEGINNING

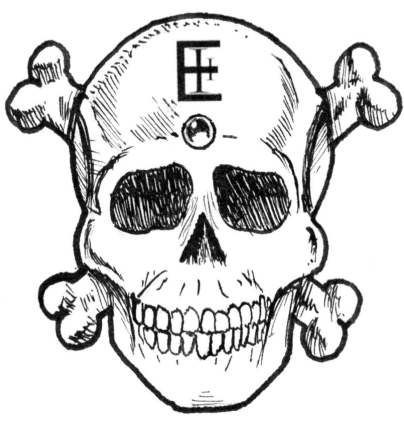

To Know - To Will
To Dare - To Be Silent